TAKE HEART

TAKE HEART

POEMS BY MOLLY PEACOCK

VINTAGE BOOKS

A DIVISION OF RANDOM HOUSE, INC.

NEW YORK

FOR MARC-ANTONIO CONSOLI
AND JOAN STEIN

First Vintage Books edition, April 1989
Copyright © 1984, 1985, 1986, 1987, 1988, 1989 by Molly Peacock
All rights reserved under International and Pan-American Copyright
Conventions. Published in the United States by Random House, Inc.,
New York, and simultaneously in Canada by Random House of
Canada Limited, Toronto.

I would like to thank the Ingram Merrill Foundation, Yaddo, the
MacDowell Colony, and Friends Seminary for support that allowed me
the time to complete this book; and to thank Phillis Levin and
Miranda Sherwin for their insight and help with the final manuscript.

*Poems in this volume first appeared, often in earlier versions and with other
titles, in the following periodicals:*
Boulevard, Cover Arts (New York), *Graham House Review, Leadings: A
Miscellany from Friends, Michigan Quarterly Review, The Missouri Review,
The Paris Review, Pequod, Poetry East, Seneca Review, Sequoia, Shenandoah,*
and *Southwest Review.*

"Good Girl," and "Throwing Out Old Clothes" (published as "Don't
Fix It Again") were first published in *The Nation.*

"Commands of Love," "Prayer," "The Ghost" (published as "The
Choice"), "The Spell," "A Simple Purchase" and "When I Love You"
were first published in *Poetry.*

Library of Congress Cataloging-in-Publication Data

Peacock, Molly
  Take heart.

  I. Title.
PS3566.E15T3 1989b 811'.54 88-26463
ISBN 0-679-72196-7 (pbk.)

Manufactured in the United States of America
98765432
First Edition

CONTENTS

TAKE HEART

HOW I COME TO YOU

Even a rock
has insides.
Smash one and see
how the shock

reveals the rough
dismantled gut
of a thing once dense.
Making the cut

into yourself,
maybe you hoped
for rock solid through.
That hope I hoped,

too. Dashed
on my rocks was my wish
of what I was. Angry,
dense and mulish,

I smashed myself
and found my heart
a cave, ready to be
lived in. A start,

veined, unmined.
This is how I come to you:
broken,
not what I knew.

THE VALLEY OF THE MONSTERS

You might think I'm going to tell you where I've been,
but I'm writing about where I haven't been,

as yet. The Valley of the Monsters is a real place
where rocks are formed in monsters' shapes,

as clouds take the shapes people point to in the sky—
only the rocks, of course, are more permanent. To say why

I'm writing audaciously about what I haven't seen
will occupy the rest of my life this poem: the scene

is a kitchen where two dinosaurs, the kind with those little
lizardy hands and huge haunches, stand in the middle

of the floor guzzling beer and crushing the cans
with their scaly thumb-equivalents. Hah! I *can*

be audacious because I've been here before! I see
it's the Valley of the Monsters of my drunken family!

In fact, I grew up in the Valley of the Monsters, where
minds were formed in monsters' shapes, like what air

currents turn clouds into, shapes in the sky people point at,
feeling lucky to have grasped the fragmentary, but

the minds of the monsters are far more permanent.
The rocks that form the real Valley of the Monsters are meant

to be paid for as a tourist attraction, whereas of course
my dinosaurs with beer cans are a matter of the coarse

substance of unpaid life. The curious thing about expression
is that the simple telling of something begins the motion

of fulfilling the need to say it. Thus it is healthy
to speak, even in rhymes, about where we see

we're going, even if we haven't been there to find
our answer yet. The rocks are quite permanent, I find,

as is the need to expose them to the fantasy
of finding shapes in them, for fantasy is scrutiny.

BUFFALO

Many times I wait there for my father,
in parking lots of bars or in the bars
themselves, drinking a cherry Coke, Father
joking with a bartender who ignores
him, except to take the orders. I think
of the horrible discipline of bartenders,
and how they must feel to serve, how some shrink
from any conversation to endure
the serving, serving, serving of disease.
I think I would be one of these, eternally
hunched around myself, turning to appease
monosyllabically in the dimness. To flee
enforced darkness in the afternoon
wasn't possible, where was I to go?
Home was too far to walk to, my balloon,
wrinkling in the front seat in the cold, too
awful to go out and play with. Many
times I wait there for Daddy, stupefied
with helpless rage. *Looks old for her age,* any
one of the bartenders said. Outside, the wide
endlessly horizontal vista raged
with sun and snow: it was Buffalo, gleaming
below Great Lakes. Behind bar blinds we were caged,
some motes of sunlight cathedrally beaming.

COMMANDS OF LOVE

The tragedy of a face in pain
is how little you can do for it
because it is so closed. Having lain

outlined in knives, afraid to move,
it cannot move and therefore cannot love.
This is why we say it is a mask,

for the face is so frozen by hurt and fear
it is unable to ask for help.
You can do nothing but stay near.

This is why we hover over those in pain
doing things unasked for and unwanted,
hoping simply with our bodies to cover pain

as if to protect it. Better to go away.
But by asking for help pain is erased,
for the face opens to say what it has to say

and a beauty of concentration overcomes it.
The pain is saying outwardly what it is.
The help it asks for is what overcomes it.

Help me on with this dress.
Get me a glass of water.
Look, I've made a mess.

Both the face of pain and the face of the one
riveted to it in relief believe there's still
something to get, something to be done.

SAY YOU LOVE ME

What happened earlier I'm not sure of.
Of course he was drunk, but often he was.
His face looked like a ham on a hook above

me—I was pinned to the chair because
he'd hunkered over me with arms like jaws
pried open by the chair arms. "Do you love

me?" he began to sob. "Say you love me!"
I held out. I was probably fifteen.
What had happened? Had my mother—had she

said or done something? Or had he just been
drinking too long after work? "He'll get *mean,*"
my sister hissed, "just *tell* him." I brought my knee

up to kick him, but was too scared. Nothing
could have got the words out of me then. Rage
shut me up, yet "DO YOU?" was beginning

to peel, as of live layers of skin, age
from age from age from him until he gazed
through hysteria as a wet baby thing

repeating, "Do you love me? Say you do,"
in baby chokes, only loud, for they came
from a man. There wouldn't be a rescue

from my mother, still at work. The same
choking sobs said, "Love me, love me," and my game
was breaking down because I couldn't do

anything, not escape into my own
refusal, *I won't, I won't,* not fantasize
a kind, rich father, not fill the narrowed zone,

empty except for confusion until the size
of my fear ballooned as I saw his eyes,
blurred, taurean—my sister screamed—unknown,

unknown to me, a voice rose and leveled
off, "I love you," I said. *"Say 'I love you,
Dad!' "* "I love you, Dad," I whispered, leveled

by defeat into a cardboard image, untrue,
unbending. I was surprised I could move
as I did to get up, but he stayed, burled

onto the chair—my monstrous fear—she screamed,
my sister, "Dad, the phone! Go answer it!"
The phone wasn't ringing, yet he seemed

to move toward it, and I ran. He had a fit—
"It's not ringing!"—but I was at the edge of it
as he collapsed into the chair and blamed

both of us at a distance. No, the phone
was not ringing. There was no world out there,
so there we remained, completely alone.

BLANK PAPER

Blank sheets of paper were my inheritance.
A plain envelope below my uncle's face,
my dead father's life in legal miniature:
the paper nowhere mentioned my name. Erased,

vanishing as the ink had vanished,
I crept from the couch where I slept, TV
still on to morning cartoons, just outlines
of people, as I was, blank inside. To be

was to be denied. I nearly laid my head
on the open oven door, but it was messy
with meat juice and baked-on drips of sauces
I had made when alive. I held me,

rocking my outline below the TV,
where I watched the cartoons from the floor as
I had as a little girl, my father
blacked out on the couch. Now blank paper has

the life I tried to restore there, after
feeling I was nothing. The feeling, too,
is my inheritance, but the true gift
is to re-create all the old anew:

My head on an oven door just repeated
the way I was disinherited. For him to give
me my life long ago was what I needed,
thus what I write both re-blankens my life
and fills it in with a right to live.

DREAM COME TRUE

The little girl is shy.
She wonders why
on tiptoes, like paws,
there are laws

such as these:
she will never please
however much
she curtsies, never touch

except the dead head
she touches now and
springs away from, knocking
the flowers, ripping her stocking

on the casket that is
so much higher than she is.
She gets nothing
because there is nothing

but pale flowers on a waxed floor,
no more "Stop that!" then no more.
Her father who lies there
will be her nightmare.

UNEXPECTED FREEDOM

The aftermath of death is a release
to finally grow away from the one
who stunted you. Now you get enough sun.
The aftermath of death is a release
from drunken midnight calls and the unceasing
responsibility without control
of the one who stunted you. You'll feel you stole
this freedom that will in fact come to appease
the unceasing need you have to expand
in the aftermath of death. The release
is the fact that the dead stay dead, thank God, and
you are free now to live until you die,
nourished just by the fact that you're alive
in the aftermath and now you rest in peace.

PUTTING A BURDEN DOWN

Putting a burden down feels so empty
you almost want to hoist it up again,
for to carry nothing means there is no "me"

almost. Then freedom, like air, creeps in
as into a nearly airtight house, estranging
you and your burden, making a breach to leap in,

changing an airless place into a landscape,
an outdoors so full of air it leaves you breathless,
there's so much to breathe. Now you escape

what you didn't even know had held you.
It's so big, the outside! How will you ever carry it?
No, no, no, you are only meant to live in it.

This wide plain infused with a sunset? Here?
With distant mountains and a glittering sea?
With distant burdens and a glittering "me," here.

THAT LEAF

That leaf tries very hard to turn over
in very little wind. It lifts a corner
and settles on the ground exhausted, lifts
itself half over but, as the wind shifts,
falls face down eating mud. It hikes half up
in an attitude of prayer, then gives up.
Suddenly it turns fully over, sun
illuminating its dry belly. The sum
of all attempts is change, yet when change comes
it's finally so easy the world becomes
instantly rearranged, present
from past estranged, the old energy spent
in almost angry astonishment.
All the leaf sees is sky, appallingly wide,
though it always was so—depleted, terrified
by sudden perspective, the outside brought inside,
though it always was so.

BLUE AND HUGE

The ocean's great to look at
because there's enough of it.
It's like music, a substance that

can't be cut up. It has no pit
to stymie a knife. It's like true laughter:
even laugh-o-meters can't measure it.

You can't divide it in half, sure
to subdivide it in tracts.
Like scent, this way it will waft, or

that, diminished, but in fact
not divided. All
in the world can watch: it will wax

and ebb for everyone.
It will crash on the beach, smell
acrid with brine, being for everyone

HUGE. It's blue enough so all can tell
there's blue enough. In this respect it is
not like love, not like a till

full of dollar bills, not like a kiss
or even many kisses, not
like food, like days, like jobs. It is

indivisibly vast and sufficient. What
else is like it? I can't think, for
I am busy dividing: cut, cut.

Poverty says divide, not provide for.
It splits the core.

MONEY

Money is viscous in states of resistance
and runs fastest when given a wintery
attention, as of an ice cliff's eye toward a source
of a river birthing far below, or the glance
a puffin on its floe gives a fish:
quick beak. Money is viscous when heated
by desire, like old gum spat on street tar:
it's on your shoe, it's on everything you do.
You can't get it off till you cool, yes, you,
whose name is Volcano, nickname: Too-Hot-To-Handle.
These are the properties of money, as if
it were an element on the periodic chart:
—a gluey solid when hotly fixed on
—liquid in cold's distant, minute attention
—immobile when taking part of your warmth
—running like water, or time, when held apart.

PAINTED DESERT

Connivers are the victims I hate most,
feeling close to them in mindset. Take this
Navaho below his sign, "See Live Pet Wolf."
Oh, the wolf is there all right, chained, while his
loose Doberman torments it in the sun
of the empty Painted Desert, nothing
but my friend, me, and this salesman moving
beneath the lean-to's shadow: he has won.
I'm paying him for a silver bracelet.
His body is toughly beautiful, like those
of women on the porn channel who let
cameras massage their sex as they close,
almost, their eyes. It makes their faces sly.
Hate his vapid cleverness: see a child
surviving adult cruelty with a mild
deserted face on a humming body.
Wanting craft, I get the world, dry, shoddy
and expensive below the sky, expansive.

THE SPELL

The job in certain lives has been to find **A**
way to live with feeling—for just to **B**
the selves they are requires them to **C**
things they were forbidden to. All the **D**
structive or delicious forces became in**E**
luctable vapors inside the in**F**
able masks of personal traits the wee**G**
boards of their parents created. But their n**H**
ures were disguised, not destroyed.

          I
have the same job in my life, avoiding the **J**-
hook of Things Not To Say, not to *know* (not ris**K**
things, but life-threatening ones, with their deep w**L**
of being unloved and unforgiven). **M**
pathy was my way out. My mother wouldn't ev**N**
feel anything; she actually unlearned how to (th**O**
feeling what everyone else felt was simply **P**
nal servitude).

      Generations got this **Q**
from generations: Don't say what you feel, *you* **R**
not you. Generations of liars in a m**S**
one got the next one into became a **T**
leology of undoing. *You are not U,*
you must hide what you feel. Behind your **V**
nial mask you must hide, you as a **W**,
as spelling masks meaning, a kind of h**X**
on the alphabet, created to cover **Y**,
not to destroy it, but to make it ha**Z**.

A HOT DAY IN AGRIGENTO

Temples look like discarded alphabets.
We loved lying in their shadows lazily
deciphering and resting and laying bets

on what they really were for. Easily
caught by fantasy, we no longer cared
why they were there, just *that* they were. Happy

to sit down and drink the water we shared
(having lugged our plastic bottle, and hats,
and camera, through the human dung bared

right there in the sun—where else could you get
relief with no toilets?) we guzzled it down
and splashed it on our arms, hands, legs, and necks.

A girl in dirty, expensive clothes found
us with the bottle and asked us for some.
I said no. As she left, a gagging smell wound

its way out from the bottle's damp lung.
I've often been asked to give what I've saved,
but under the temple I said no, numbed

against the girl, like one of those bridesmaids
who kept her oil in the Bible story
and was safe for the night. I'd hated those maids

until I became one in *my* story,
the shape of the character I'd searched for
surprising me as the temples did: See

how golden but pocked they've become, nor
are they quite decipherable anymore,
at least to those who forget what they're for,

which is worship, the greed of prayer.
"So that's who you are," my friend said. "Thirsty?"
With him I drank, not quite the maid in the story,

but in her shadow, like letters at rest
in new words on a palimpsest.

THE SURGE

Maybe it is the shyness of the pride
he has when he puts my hand down to feel
the hardness of his cock I hadn't tried

by any conscious gesture to raise,
yet it rose for my soft presence in the bed:
there was nothing I did to earn its praise

but be alive next to it. Maybe it is
the softness of want beneath his delight
at his body going on without his . . .

his will, really, his instructions . . . that
surges inside me as a sort of surrender
to the fact that I am, that I was made, that

there is nothing I need do to please but be.
To do nothing but be, and thus be wanted:
so, this is love. *Look what happened,* he says as he

watches my hand draw out what it did not raise,
purpled in sleep. The surge inside me must
come from inside me, where the world lies,

just as the prick stiffened to amaze us
came from a rising inside him. The blessing
we feel is knowing that *out there* is nothing.
The world inside us has come to praise us.

PRAYER

Herbie sat the class down and told us how,
Only when you really love someone, you'd
Let the car idle, hold hands, and pray on
Dates instead of necking. How sexy to be
In Sunday School class hunched with girl-chasing,
Necking-prone boys and boy-crazy Christian
Girls cajoled, attended to, by Herbie.

Here's the church, here's the steeple, open the doors,
And see the people—a game taught children to
Numb them into sitting during sermons.
Doing this simply focused the wiggling.
So prayer on dates focuses the writhing.

I love to hold your hand in church under-
Neath the weight of our bowed heads in stained light.

Chasing through our minds over terrible
Hurdles are our problems, which we whisper
Under our breaths as prayer. Our bodies
Roll slightly side to side, beneath the beliefs of
Centuries pressed. Herbie extolled the holding of
Hands in church, *if you really love the man.*

Now see the spirit writhe where bodies writhed,
Our prayer dangerous, as our play was, for
When we hold hands now, it is as necessary:
     flesh is still the church.

PARROTS OF THE WORLD

"Parrots of the World,"
a street-level shop flush with the other
street-level shops in a one-level village
lying like a flag furled

into a long skinny box
(one end at the train station, the other
at an inlet of ocean) was unnoticeable.
We missed it twice, a blue box

on a street of blue shops
tilted toward the turquoise ocean. It's not here,
my love said. It must be, the phone book said so,
I said, noticing the tops

of two macaws' heads
behind a window I'd seen just our own heads
reflected in twice before. (But before we go in,
I've got to tell you, *insteads*

filled my own life
with the blank regularity that these shops
fill their street—many unnoticeable somethings *instead*
of what in my life

I desired.) I desire *this,*
I thought to myself as I looked at my lover
holding the shop door. Under the hanging cages
I gave him a kiss.

He was shyly embarrassed,
and I was pleased. The boy behind the counter
gave me a small parrot to make friends with—
a chartreuse candy kiss

nibbling on my sundress.
Before I buy the bird, I've got to tell you
we'd been lying, one's head on the other's lap
in tanned undress

for hours on the beach.
Our shoulders smelled of salt; our tongues, from kissing,
didn't know whose mouth they belonged in.
All this within reach.

I love to watch you buy things,
my lover said. The bird was scrabbling up his shirt.
It was so tame, it came to both our fingers.
I grinned beneath the wings

of cockatoos, cockatiels,
Amazon parrots, African parrots, finches, toucans,
    macaws,
and wrote a big check, and learned about the habits
of my new pet. It feels,

I said, no *I* feel happy!
I love to watch you coddle that animal,
my love said, What will you call it? I didn't know.
He said, Call it Happy.

Before I call it Happy,
I should tell you we fell in love so slowly,
past years escarped by insteads. What's its name?
the salesman said. I said Happy.

FOOD FOR TALK

The bird delights in human food,
claw clamped to the lip of the cup,
and I delight in human good
the way the bird delights in food,
soft and foreign to its beak, wooed
by something not its own abrupt
crack of the seed. So human good
is soft law to the sharp lip's cup.

JOY

Joy seeps. It's not
the hot sporadic light
that siblings fight
for, or the shot

the deprived demand,
the hot want of Big Love.
It doesn't glove
a feeling hand,

it *is* the feeling
in the hand, like light seeping,
blood transfusing
like light infusing

slow, accreted,
time almost defeated
in its outline,
as lights outline

shadows. Joy goes
at the pace water flows,
a voluptuous sameness
of wave, shameless

because it is not
the end of desire. It does not
cover a cold
corpse of need, or fold

up childhood. Void
of "answer to" or "purpose of,"
joy is the void
that aimless love

diffuses into,
seeking a level, as light
fills up a night
spilling morning into.

MY GOD, WHY ARE YOU CRYING?

When someone cries, after making love spills
a pail of tears inside, it is the ache
of years, all the early years' emptiness
hollowed into a pail-like form which fills
with feeling now felt aloud, that resounds.

Why would an orgasm make someone weep?
Why, for being loved now when one had not been.
The anger tendered into tears astounds
the lover with fear to have struck so deep.

MERELY BY WILDERNESS

The breasts enlarge, and a sweet white discharge
coats the vaginal lips. The nipples itch.
A five-week fetus in the uterus,
the larger share of a large soft pear,
soaks quietly there. Should I run directly
and insist that he marry me? Resist
is what we do. It is this: I'm in what
I never thought I'd be caught in,
and it's a strong net, a roomy deluxe net,
the size of civilization. To shun
this little baby—how can I? Maybe
I could go it alone, fix us a home,
never seem to ask why inside the dream
we'd not look beyond, so not ask beyond:
a poor scratch-castle with a beat-in door.
I can't do this alone, yet I am so alone
no one, not even this child inside me, even
the me I was, can feel the wild cold buzz
that presses me into this place, bleakness
that will break me, except I cannot be
broken merely by wilderness, I can only
be lost.

CHRISEASTER

I woke up to the bleating of a lamb
in the garagelike recovery room
crowded with wheeled beds waiting to be parked. "Am
I?" I asked as I began to disentomb

myself from the anesthesia, "where I am?"
Why is there a lamb in this garagelike farm?
Something was wrong in the barn. The nervous bleat-cry
continued. When I raised my head in alarm

and saw the green hospital interior
and felt the blood between my legs and was
frightened, I thought, "It is not hygenic to store
a lamb in here!" Of course the bleating I heard was

a baby crying helplessly way down the room.
I had had an abortion and the baby crying
was someone else's, yet mine—the world was a womb
and the room was still a barn. Lying

back in my stupor in the manger, "ChrisEaster,"
I thought, for it was Eastertime, but I had
condensed the birth and death that were
usually separated by seasons as I bled,

then closed my eyes sarcophagally.
Oh yes, the lamb was the Lamb of God, bleating
in hunger and terror in the tomb room, all woolly
and soft with human pain. My heart lay beating

steadily, for I was alive. Marc stood weeping
in the hall, and later watched as I lay sleeping
in the manger, on the bald hill, near the tomb
at home.

ON THE STREET

A curette has the shape of a grapefruit spoon.
They dilate the cervix, then clean out the womb
with the jagged prow, just like separating
the grapefruit from its skin, although the softening
yellow rind won't bear another fruit and
. . . and this womb will? Well, this womb *can,*
if two will. Oh, I am sick of will and all
unconscious life! I am sick of the Fall
and the history of human emotion!
Who knows the end of our commotion except
God, the novelist? Once my heart leapt straight
from its socket say-beating, *Change Your Fate,*
yet I found in order to live my heart
had to beat back in its own pocket: the start
of change ending by continuing living
with wet possibility lingering
like a light rain glazing our separate
apartment buildings now where, unpregnant,
unmarried, and with no one to worry over
us in our old age as we were sure this never-
born child would, we don our raincoats and goofily
smile under our umbrellas, unceasingly
happy to see each other when we meet,
on the street.

THE GHOST

The ghost of my pregnancy, a large
amorphous vapor, much larger than me,
comes when I am alarmed to comfort me,
though it, too, alarms me, and I dodge

away saying, "Leave me alone"; and the ghost,
always beneficent, says, "You're a tough one
to do things for." The ghost must have done
this lots, it so completely knows I'm lost

and empty. It returns the fullness and slow
connection to all the world as it is.
When I let it surround me, the embrace is
more mother than baby. How often we don't know

the difference. It's not a dead little thing
without a spinal cord yet, but a spirit of
the parent we all ought to have had, of
possibility. "I was meant to be dead." Thinking

why it said it was *meant* to be dead brings
the tangible comfort: how I used the fetus
shamelessly, how the brief pregnancy showed us,
its father and me, these choices, not shriveling

but choice alive with choice, for as our brief
parenthood dislodged our parents' anchor
and set us anxiously adrift, more
of our lost natures appeared. In my grief,

I never say good-bye to the ghost, for
I've forgotten it's been there. That's what it's for.
The thought of my pregnancy somehow unmoors
the anxiety the choice still harbors.

THINGS CAN BE NAMED TO DEATH

Things can be named to death,
you know, by talking
about them too much:
as if you were walking

past the same lamppost
again and again
nearly erasing it
by moving past it: ten

times in your trenchcoat
past the diffused light
of the lamp in the rain:
in your mental trenchcoat

the lamppost a feeling
you're merely moving past
while concentrating
on something falsely *else:* last

night, last year, last rain,
the lamppost a real god
behind a false god's name
being named and renamed.

A SIMPLE PURCHASE

Buying flowers
lowers
panic levels
as bevels
in mirrors
reduce terrors
by taking
images
and breaking
their edges:

freely
buds of peonies
burst from stems
beyond the whims
of the devil.
Flowers are not evil,
though they make belief
in evil easy:
they're so beautiful
that God must be ugly.

They're not in His image,
but what He wants to be.
He sets as His wage
what He wants to see,
for He is cancerous,
crippled,
leprous,
and pulled
toward terror.
God must be error

incarnate!
How else can we account
for evil and still mount
our belief? Hate
must be His state.
Our damage
isn't in God's eye,
but God's *eye.*
It's His image,
the one He creates in,

a state of sin.
Thus the terror around us
surrounds us
because it is God.
Here I thought He was good.
He can barely lift
His scaled hand
to His bulbous forehead
or, for the sores, shift
from side to side.

Not to hide
what He is, but
to gain what
He would be,
He must make beauty,
just as we hope
to change—and grope
toward form in our lives,
even if only the rhymes

of our mistakes survive.
Thus all is pattern.
The continual figure
of a leaf
is the flower
of error and belief
in the world's faults
which are God's faults:
horror
in order.

HOW I HAD TO ACT

One day I went and bought a fake fur coat
from two old ladies in a discount shop
no young woman should have walked into: taupe

fluff with leopard spots for four hundred bucks
which I charged—no cash till my paycheck—
admired by the two old saleslady crooks.

Five minutes later I was at my shrink's
casually shoving the bag by a chair,
one arm flopping out synthetically. Trinkets,

all belonging to my crooked grandmother,
floated across the wall already filled with the shrink's
trinkets. Afterwards, among the minks

on the street, I caught sight of my grandmother
in a shopwindow. The wind was howling.
I wore the fake coat with a babushka. Another

possibility was: that was *me.* I didn't
have four hundred dollars and felt humiliated
by what I had acted out and berated

myself for buying a blazer in the size
of my sister the week before! You MESS!
I called myself a lot of names. Eyes

on the bus looked up when I barreled on
in the coat I couldn't return to the store.
I refused to go shopping alone anymore.

My rich friend said, "A fun fur . . . how daring."
How daring to become my clever, lying
grandmother and before that my sister, whose loved,

dirty stuffed leopard Gram craftily destroyed.
I had promised myself a real fur coat
which I wanted as I did a real self, employed

with real feelings. Instead I bought a fake
which I couldn't afford. "What a mistake!"
I chortled to my shrink, who agreed,

though I did not want her to. How terrible,
I wanted her to say, How terrible
you have to act this way.

ANGER SWEETENED

What we don't forget is what we don't say.
I mourn the leaps of anger covered
by quizzical looks, grasshoppers covered
by coagulating chocolate. Each word,
like a leggy thing that would have sprung away,
we caught and candified so it would stay
spindly and alarmed, poised in our presence,
dead, but in the shape of its old essence.
We must eat them now. We must eat the words
we should have let go but preserved, thinking
to hide them. They were as small as insects blinking
in our hands, but now they are stiff and shirred
with sweet to twice their size, so what we gagged
will gag us now that we are so enraged.

THE DEFECT-O-METER

The healthy can listen in if they want
but the defect-o-meter is for us.
Its flash-quick scale, hair-triggered and ruthless,
burns our spirit when we get what we want,
just like an old man heating up pennies
atop a woodstove, "Heh, heh." He asks children,
"You want a penny? Heh, heh." Unlike him,
the defect-o-meter doesn't laugh and wheeze
maniacally when we burn. It remains silent,
implacably machinelike, raising mirrors
to our burned spirits where we see our cores
ooze with a blue-reddish substance. It's meant
to show us how defective we are just
when we've achieved—oh, anything, money,
a lover at the door, plane tickets. . . . Our knees,
our spiritual knees—or is it *needs*—must
be a mass of scabs from being brought to them
hourly, daily, until we are infirm.
Yet where are our wheelchairs? Perhaps if we just
shifted ourselves into one of our arms,
leaving one arm free (for we are holding
ourselves in pain) we could use that arm to swing
a bat into the eye of the meter! Alarms
go off, but who comes running? There's only us!
Smash it! Smash it! There's only us.
Plane tickets, money, and first the pink nails,
then the loved hands rush out, and no siren wails.

FEELING SORRY FOR YOURSELF

Feeling sorry for yourself is the right
thing to do, the moral and human thing,
for it takes you beyond contempt. One night
you may remember an embarrassing
thing you've done (mine, stupidly, was having
a near-affair with my friend's husband when we
were in our twenties) and find yourself masking
what you were with hatred. That word, "stupidly,"
was my remnant of self-hatred. The affair
was never consummated; it was an
elaborately withheld romance. To repair
a self *requires* feeling sorry for it. Can
contempt clarify the way sorrow can?
It's clear to me I was so hungry then,
and I am sorry to have lost the friend
and sorry also that I did not eat.

THROWING OUT OLD CLOTHES

Throwing out old clothes is painful, because
how do I know I won't need them again?
This one, discolored under the arms, was
worn to dinner—roast duck—with two old friends.
It smells creaky, like floorboards smell; the closet
where it's been jammed smells of bits of stain (duck
à l'orange, crab, pork, veal) dried, pressed, and set
into now-napless cloth. Time to chuck
the lot. What I need again are the friends,
not the clothes, though *they* were friends. One woman
moved back to her hometown and remarried.
That one I sewed, then let fray to the ends.
The deeper friend cast me off for a man.
That friendship—like what to wear when hurried
by one's schedule, the satisfying skirt
one grabs, for it fits and fits till it bags—hurt
not to fix. Ditching loved clothes hurts because
all age does; holes like mouths sag open: *it was.*

FRIENDSHIP WITH MEN

Is friendship with men like friendship with birds?
Is friendship the way this parrot nestles
beneath my chin, its feathers only disturbed
by the regular wind from my nostrils?

Unexpectedly, another species
and I achieve intimacy: we are
each other's pets; as I imagine the seas
at a great distance are pets of the stars.

REUNION

Sweat lingering in broadcloth over soap,
the first man's smell I smell belongs to you.
Can't look at myself. I trust you see my taupe
skin on the clammy bedsheets clearer than I do.
The offseason blue snowlight in that broken-
down summer motel all college kids freeze in
I see clearer than my own skin. To look in
the mirror you are is the best I can do, woozy
with fear to see what I am. Your chest—I look there—
your moley back and neck, scaly kneecaps,
nervous groin. As worried about my hair
as what I'll do in bed, I stick a shower cap
on my head the first time we make love
ever in our lives.

        How did we stop ourselves
from talking about this? What blasphemy of
our youth we made when we talked of adult selves'
divorces, psychotherapies, and awards—
nineteen years of experienced life behind. Hoards
of things happened to us that don't make any
difference! My dear, I knew you were dying
when you called, and by waiting for you never to tell me,
I helped you engage in a form of lying
that stopped the only gift I could give you:
my half of us then, of what we know was true
but must say to be free in it, *I remember you.*

INSTEAD OF HER OWN

Instead of her own, my grandmother washed my hair.
The porcelain was cold at the back of my neck,
my fragile neck. Altogether it was cold there.

She did it so my hair would smell sweet.
What else is like the moist mouse straw
of a girl's head? Why, the feeling of complete

peace the smell brings to a room whose window
off oily Lake Erie is rimmed with snow.
Knuckles rasping at young temples know,

in the involuntary way a body knows,
that as old is, so young grows. Completion
drives us: substitution is our mission.

Thin little head below thin little head grown old.
Water almost warm in a room almost cold.

FRIENDS

Friends are our families now. They act
with rivalry and concern, as sisters
and brothers have acted. They repeat the fact
of family without the far-walked blisters
of heredity. Friends echo childhood
but stop childish acts, for they do not require
the child in us to serve. It is our mood
that friends serve and in our mirrors we admire
their faces and ours. Where would I meet
my sister as a friend now? Though I love her,
we have only our childhoods in common.
Friends help me get rid of what we'll never
get rid of: our terror of the childhood we shun.
How sick I am of it! Yet I am it, which
my friends know, for they feel it as we embrace,
as I feel their families coursing through them. We itch
to understand what we cannot erase
but can no longer live inside of. Thus
we confide in those outside we bring beside us.

THE WORM

"There's a worm at the bottom of each bottle!"
you cried gleefully at the faculty table
I'd commandeered for my friends, having startled

the whole room by worming the table
for my depressed husband and unstable,
grimy, nonfaculty friends. *I could throttle*

my own sister, I thought as I looked at you,
a tawny albatross, eyes bright, hair wild.
Now all your rotten stories would ensue,

and I'd get nervous, me the useful, mild
young woman on the college support staff, a child
to be doing such a job, though I had raised you,

and there you were, a baby whore, regaling
my modest friends with life in Mexico,
mescal! peyote! "What's wrong with a little fling

just for the money?" you exclaimed. *Just go,*
I thought, *just leave.* But how can a burnt rose
unfurl its lips and just leave the garden? "String

the older ones along. The pay's higher!"
I'd done a terrible job on you, so of course
I took you in again. *How could you be what you are,*

I thought stonily. What beauty your coarse
words had and how beautifully your long, coarse
hair swung against your shoulders, fresh fire

in blonde toss. ". . . an ugly little beige worm
at the bottom of every bottle! I mean,
how does that worm get *in* there??" That was the warm

pebbly tone of your whiskey voice at nineteen.
I was twenty-two and dead then, slain by the fiend
of motherhood and sisterhood, the earth infirm
about my turning corpse, riddled by the worm.

TWO PEONIES: TWO GIRLS

How large their heads are! Pink and leonine,
two peonies with ruffs like lions' manes,
stand in a brass tube. And now for the *sur*
in the surreal: from a log, two heads stir.
The log, fallen and decayed, bears the shape
of the tree it was, beneath its fungal drape.
The heads are the heads of two girls nurtured
by the spongy crust of what grew naturally
upright once. They lie there horizontally
while the peonies stand erect in a tree-
shaped brass tube on a table in brilliant
domestic silence. The peonies, like lions, yet
bred till pink, like prep-school girls,
make one want to believe in nature's will,
for however bred they are, they are wild
and bring wilderness to the mild table.

But the damp heads of the two girls, one farther
pulled from the tree, as one peony head, the larger,
is also farther out, are so much in nature
that one wants to believe in God and culture:
the girls smell. Their sweat is formed of the bark,
mushroomy and manurelike, that they must eat.
Their hair clings to their heads with forest slime.
They are sticky with wet spider webs and shine,
sallowly, in the brown room formed by the trees,
a cage made of disinterested tree legs.

How small their heads are! One's so small it can't
eat through the bark like the other, who eats
one side of the log and escapes to live
in a room with a brass vase of peonies that give
the wild illusion of her and her sister.

I MUST HAVE LEARNED THIS
SOMEWHERE

I loved an old doll made of bleached
wooden beads strung into a stick figure.
When the string was pulled, the tautened limbs
reached their full extent, and a human figure,
stiff with rigor mortis, rose up.
When the string was let go, the doll collapsed
into a heap more lifelike, though it missed
its spinal cord of string. I spent hours trying
to prop it up to look more human without
pulling the string, but it sat in my hands,
bent, uncontrolled in a muscular fit
or a spasm of fear. And so for myself,
collapsed in a tangled necklace,
anger painting my stiff wooden face.
Yet now my life can hold me in its hands
as long ago I coaxed the doll in my palms
to try to sit lifelike there. My mother's hands
must long ago have offered the same balm,
though I took her for an operator
holding my string. How else could I store
such an idea of comfort as I
gave the doll, so material was its cry?

ART BUZZARDS

Nude mental life was what fed me: Arp's brass
star, a Giacometti, Jackson Pollock's scrambled
anger, the ugly yellow Christ I passed
on the way to the café where I mumbled
"cream cheese on raisin" and sat near the frozen
window. Outside were sculptures in the snow.
I was frightened by the walls' white horizon
and the braceleted women, though now I know
they were only art buzzards, as I was to be.
From high school this nude mental life took three
buses to get to. The art itself was free
as I was in the café, suffering
the arty taste of the ice cream: clove.
What began there was a kind of love, clove
of art and love of self.

                        Government sponsoring
of cheese giveaways for senior citizens
bring my mother and me here on our jaunt.
It only half surprises me that she'd want
—after standing in line for cheese in a high school—
to distract herself with thought. *Vicarrions*
were what I called art buzzards in high school.
I am so pleased to find my mother is one,
or pleased I'm able to notice at last. "That one,"

she says, "it's a beauty." Max Ernst. Then the pool
of the blue eyes of teen-age "Lady H"
next to a painting of Shakespeare's cottage.
From room to room and thus through centuries
we go, often in agreement, our taste
given a distracted history, classed
along with similar hands, feet, bodies
of nude knowledge as well as naked
bodies in common.

Picture how we are fed:
enormous birds over frozen terrain
strewn with the offal of those dead to pain,
we land and are glad of nourishment of heart.
From our beaks hang the gizzards of art.

GOOD GIRL

Hold up the universe, good girl. Hold up
the tent that is the sky of your world at which
you are the narrow center pole, good girl. Rup-
ture is the enemy. Keep all whole. The itch
to be yourself, plump and bending, below a sky
unending, held up by God forever
is denied by you as Central Control. Sever
yourself, poor false Atlas, poor "Atlesse," lie
recumbent below the sky. Nothing falls down,
except you, luscious and limited on the ground.
Holding everything up, always on your own,
creates a loneliness so profound
you are nothing but a column, good girl,
a temple ruin against a sky held up
by forces beyond you. Let yourself curl
up: a fleshy fetal figure cupped
about its own vibrant soul. You are
the universe about its pole. God's not far.

DON'T THINK GOVERNMENTS
END THE WORLD

Don't think governments end the world. The blast,
the burnings, and the final famine will
be brought on *by mistake.* "I'm sorry," the last
anxious man at the control panel will
try to say, his face streaked with panic, red
hives rising on his neck. He'll have been a jerk
all his life, who couldn't get through his head
that his mother couldn't love him. Work
at the panel would give him the control
that she had denied him again and again.

Thus the world will burn through the central hole
of his being. He won't really be sure—again,
having never been assured of her—of what
he is supposed to do. That is, he'll be sure
at every exercise until the shut
blank door of the final moment injures
his gerrybuilt control and **BANG, BANG, BANG.**

It won't be his fault, his childish mother's fault,
or the fault of what produced her or what
produced what produced her back through the vault
of savage centuries. If he'd just known what,
he'd have done it to please. He might have known himself
through what he'd felt, and thus might be clear.
She might have said, "That's nice, dear,"
and we wouldn't be dead.

Aren't you scared of your life in his hands?
But of all the men whose hands you'd hope to be in,
name the one you're sure of. The history of nations
is cold; the world burns by generations.

CHOICE

To become conscious of all around us
or to live in watery, unconscious worlds
is the only choice guaranteed us
by creation. Punishments of words,
enslavement, beatings, illnesses, debt, and all
else that murder a self do not murder
our choice: which is *to know, to feel,* or fall
down the endless dreamlike tunnel in world-blur.
The pain is just the same either way.
Choice makes nothing go away.
To know just what we're born to is all
we know of why we live and to deny
our choice will kill what freedom we might feel.

WHEN I LOVE YOU

When I get on the plane, alone again
after being pressed and pulled, and lean my head
against the window until someone bangs
a briefcase into the next seat, your hands
sometimes come to rest on my cheek and head,
turning my real face toward invisible you
waiting in New York, hands flatly tender
as the wing tips of an angel's hands—you
are an angel momentarily, treating
my wound of love. Then I feel, to a depth rendered
painful in my exhaustion, a retreating
into a love of your love that moves me
as the plane gathers itself,

                    but the bulk
of someone next to me removes your hands,
for I am required to shift. As, invisibly,
they disappear, I am left with the fully adult
knowledge of my vacant self in your absence
and sit alert, but overpowered by the span
of distance between us, and by all spans:
that of your hands and that of our lives.
When I love you with a feeling of breaking
apart as the plane breaks from earth,
all is in fragments: the wingspan
of the plane bursts the angel's wingspan
which regathers as the span of love's aching
across the world's girth.

ONE PLACE

To live in one place always, like a front
of weather that hovers always above
a coast, your hopes and ideas lighting
the air over the land's head you love,
is like being in love

over years and years, the sums
of accounts and bristles of genital hairs
known and re-known, till the land
is renowned for the depths of light embossed
so deep their source seems lost.

ALTRUISM

What if we got outside ourselves and there
really was an outside out there, not just
our insides turned inside out? What if there
really were a you beyond me, not just
the waves off my own fire, like those waves off
the backyard grill you can see the next yard through,
though not well—just enough to know that off
to the right belongs to someone else, not you.
What if, when we said *I love you,* there were
a you to love as there is a yard beyond
to walk past the grill and get to? To endure
the endless walk through the self, knowing through a bond
that has no basis (for ourselves are all we know)
is altrusim: not giving, but coming to know
someone is there through the wavy vision
of the self's heat, love become a decision.

DEAR HEART

Heart, unlock yourself. Fibrillating wings,
undo your ungolding. Impoverished
by the guanoed bars' tarnish, your age sings
battened in a cage. Is that what you wished
when you planned, plotted, picked, posed and proposed
a life you imagined for yourself, a life
designed? Yet you leave your lock unsigned. Closed,
the lock's frozen dry by worry. A knife,
please. Disiridescenced heart, scrape the rust,
oxidized hysteria, from the baroque lock,
for bindings are always baroque, their trust
placed in outwitting. Security mocks
what it locks up to save. See the poor heart,
ashamed at its depletion, angel-bird
picking at soiled feathers, pulling apart
what it meant to preserve while the world occurred.

THE SMELL OF A GOD

Taking someone inside yourself (like a god,
cinnamon colored and smooth, sitting on
a tiny platform in your soul) is a process of love,
and the surest method of change. All gone
are the bumpy exteriors; essence is within
essence. The person is not a god
to be worshiped, but one alive within,
an ignorably present household god
whose being permeates your soulroom, its image
so internalized it becomes vaporized—
as an alcove, emptied, is permanently hung
with an odor of cinnamon only recognized
when its essence is present on your tongue,
as in saying something the person might say.
Genelike in soul, you two are related
so thoroughly that even when you pray
(if the real person becomes lost to you) belated
prayers for the person's presence, or even
the presence of the idol you first took in,
you are a haven of scented likeness.
And with its own peculiar nod
smilingly askew
you conjure up your god.

TRYING TO EVANGELIZE A CUT
FLOWER

Poor rose, you live a coda in a glass
coffin on a desk above the Last Will
and Testament of the desk owner. As
you are at the end of your life I will
invite you to join my religion: Church
of Limits. Join me in my gladness not
that things will end, but that we'll end the search.
The pleasure in knowing what you've got
is the love of you, and you are god. Is rage
still your prayer? No, this isn't Church of Cold
Comfort, it's your Church of Rose Comfort: walls, age,
borders, vases, all boundaries that hold
one say, "See what you've got and what you're not."
The Last Will defends its choice to the ends.
Mastery's possible within the limits
of faith in death and the practice of dearth,
little rose, life up close when the gates have closed,
Church of Limits, Church of Worth.

DEAR ARM

The only thing that's whole is our effort
to remain so. Oh arm, stop your bleeding.
Coagulated stump, deficient, embarrassing,
courting a lost hand which no longer retorts
to your blackened lip of blood, the test of faith
is a nice test to pass, and you can pass it.
It requires no manipulation, and it
demands imperfection. Unswathed, unlaced,
you enter the Land of Unwhole, a large
calmly busy place approached through wide
expanses. Here exteriors are beside
the point, for the interiors are in charge.
Your inabilities bespeak themselves
because they are what you show, wholly.
You have no hand. You cannot help be holy,
for handicapping is complete—no halves.
The test of faith is passed by being whole.
Our compensating efforts leave us full.

THERE MUST BE

There must be room in love for hate.
Allowing love to behave like a lung
allows hate in—and out. But the state

of nakedness this natural act requires,
have we the natural strength for it?
Or do we, after all our building, tire

of breathing because we are breathing so hard?
Having worked so long. Having built and rebuilt.
The four lungs in this house breathe with regard

to the continuance of our lives
and have the power to squall out the memory
of their earliest squallings, protests that survive

building and meaning. They can take love in
and breathe hate out and so manufacture
another part of the structure we determine

to live in. There must be room enough
for hate, for many rooms will be constructed
from its labor. Presume that love has room

for all other emotions, and resume, resume.

MOLLY PEACOCK was born in Buffalo, New York, in 1947, and was educated at the State University of New York at Binghamton and at The Johns Hopkins University. She is the author of two previous books of poems, *And Live Apart* and *Raw Heaven*. The poems in *Take Heart* have appeared in *The Nation*, the *Paris Review*, *Poetry* and other leading literary magazines. Molly Peacock lives in New York City, where she is a learning specialist at Friends Seminary and serves as President of the Poetry Society of America.